EASY
GUITAR
WITH NOTES & TAB

J. S. BACH
FOR EASY GUITAR

ISBN 978-1-4584-1887-6

HAL•LEONARD®
CORPORATION

7777 W. BLUEMOUND RD. P.O. BOX 13819 MILWAUKEE, WI 53213

In Australia Contact:
Hal Leonard Australia Pty. Ltd.
4 Lentara Court
Cheltenham, Victoria, 3192 Australia
Email: ausadmin@halleonard.com.au

Visit Hal Leonard Online at
www.halleonard.com

Air on the G String

from ORCHESTRAL SUITE NO. 3

By Johann Sebastian Bach

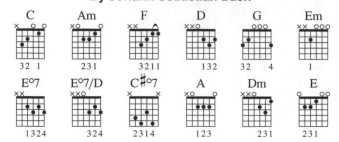

Strum Pattern: 3
Pick Pattern: 3

A

Slowly, in 2

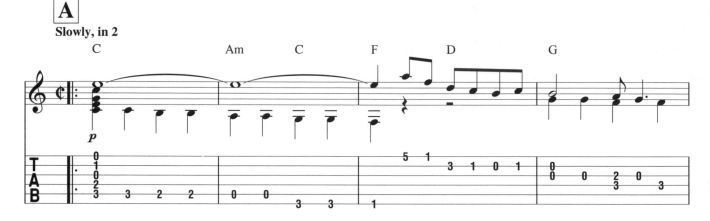

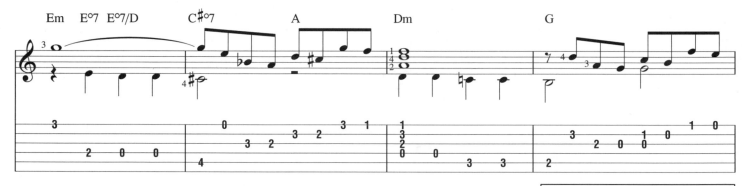

3

Aria

from THE GOLDBERG VARIATIONS

By Johann Sebastian Bach

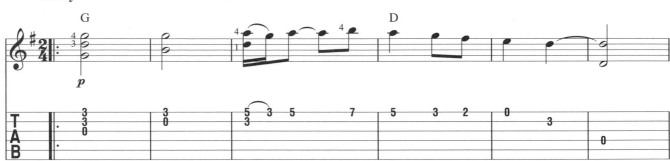

Strum Pattern: 10
Pick Pattern: 10

Slowly

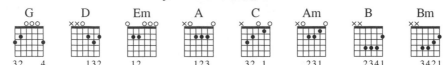

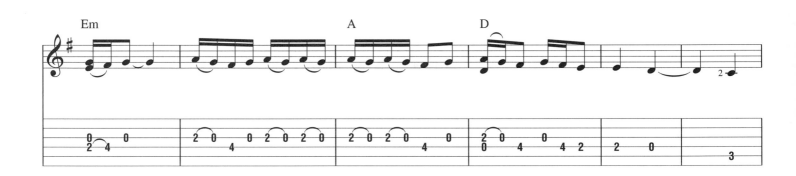

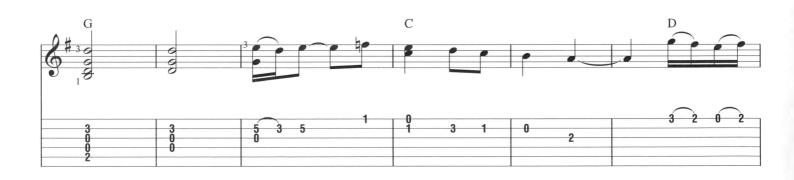

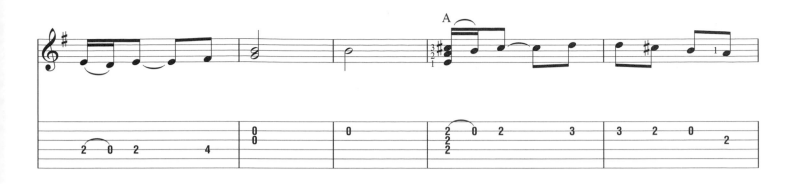

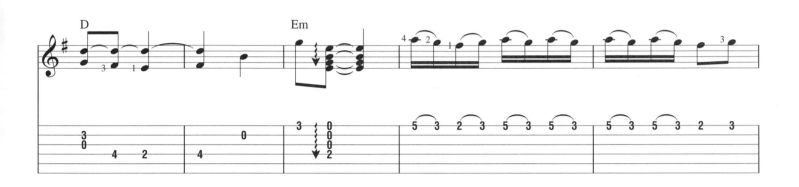

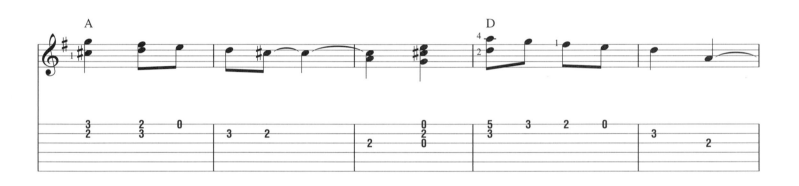

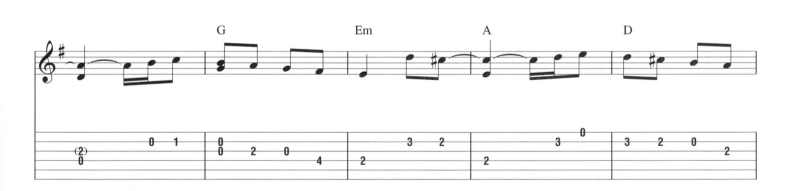

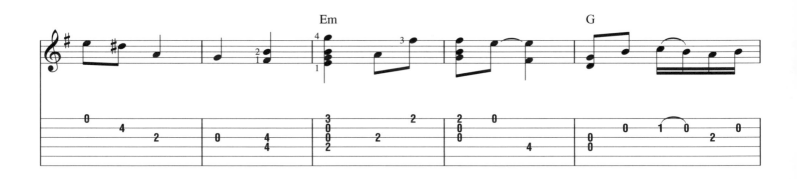

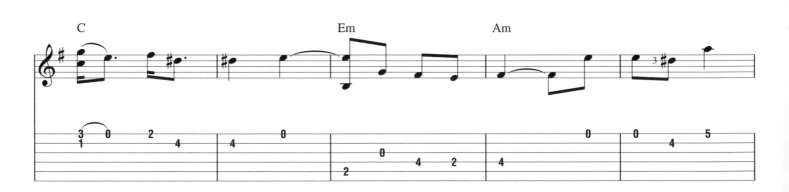

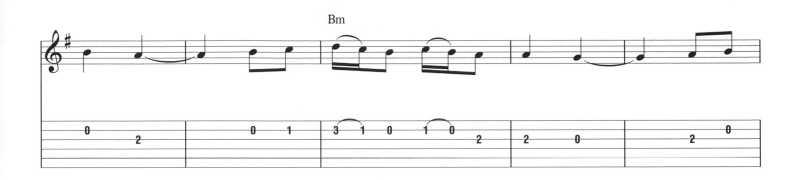

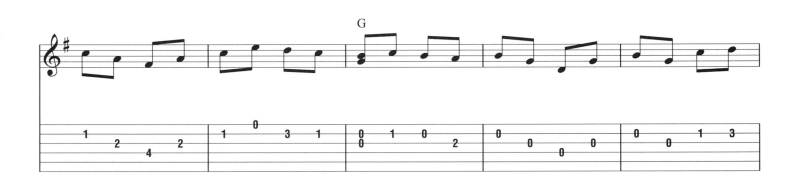

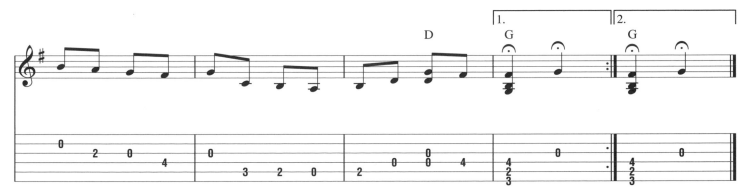

Arioso

By Johann Sebastian Bach

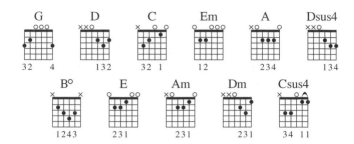

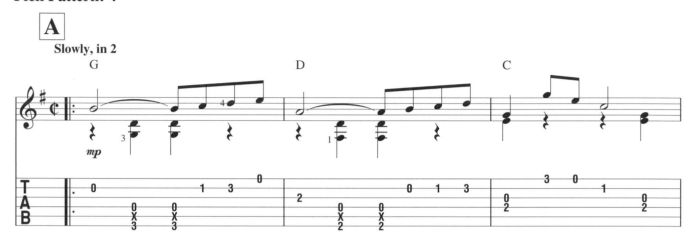

Strum Pattern: 4
Pick Pattern: 4

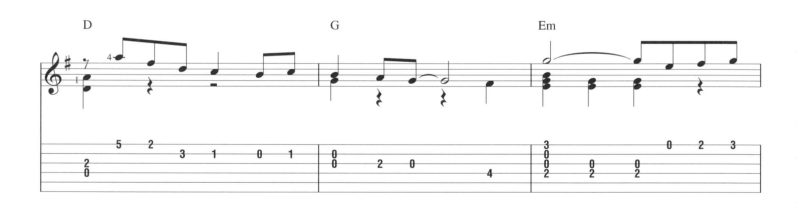

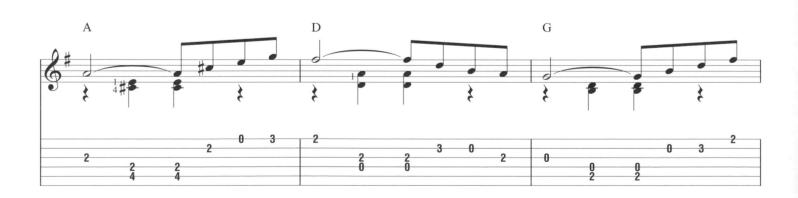

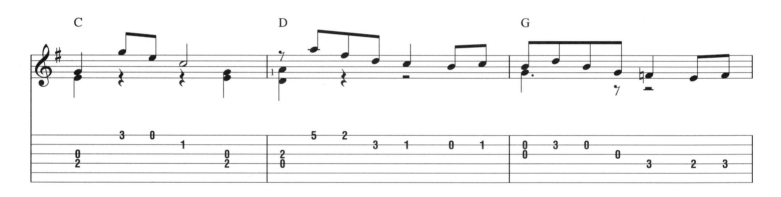

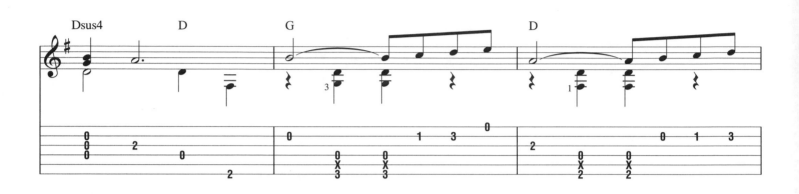

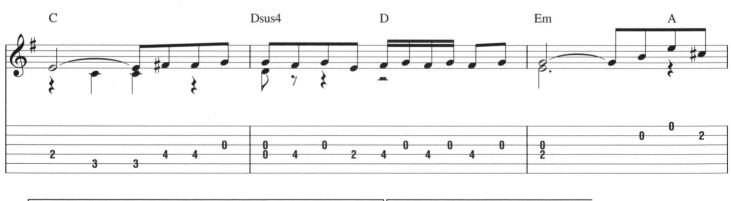

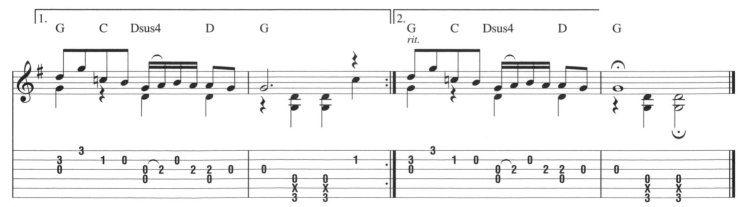

Be Thou with Me

By Johann Sebastian Bach

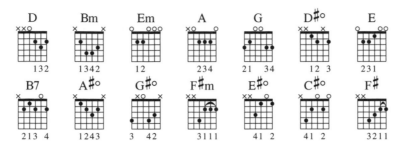

Strum Pattern: 8
Pick Pattern: 8

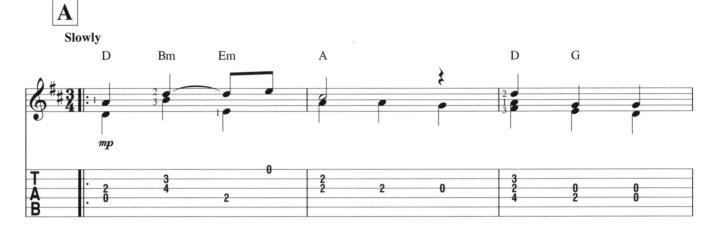

Boureé

from SUITE NO. 1 IN E MINOR FOR LUTE

By Johann Sebastian Bach

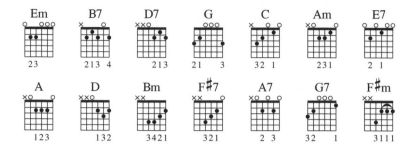

Strum Pattern: 3
Pick Pattern: 3

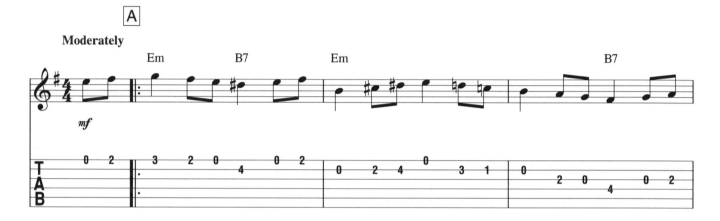

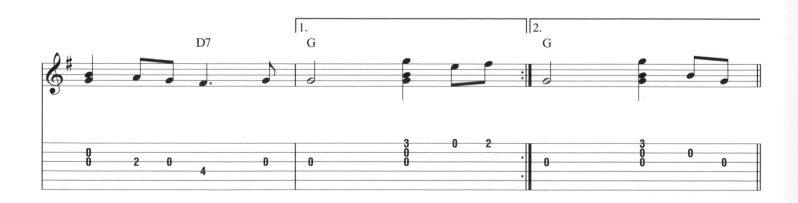

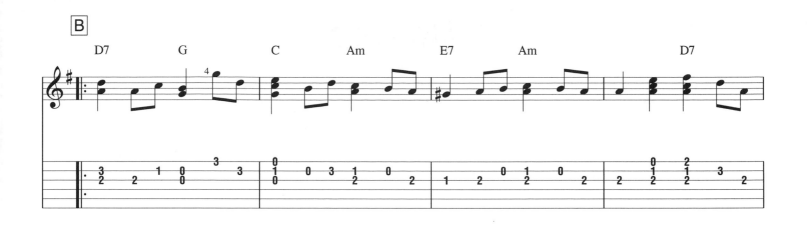

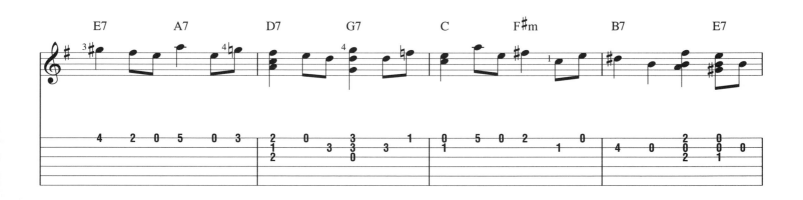

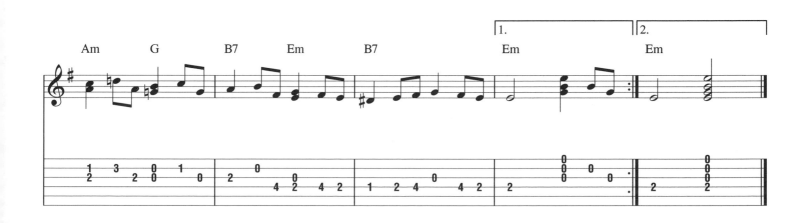

Gavotte

from PARTITA NO. 3 IN E MAJOR
By Johann Sebastian Bach

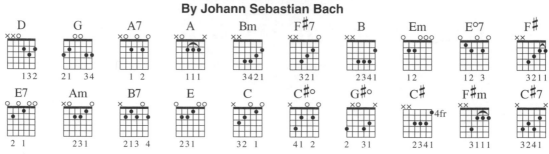

Strum Pattern: 3
Pick Pattern: 2

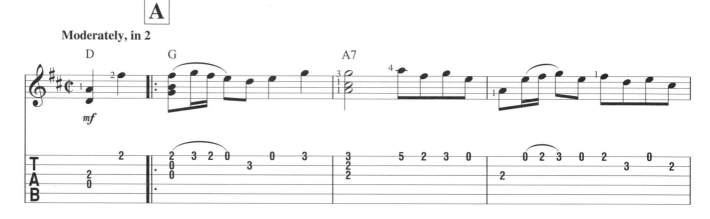

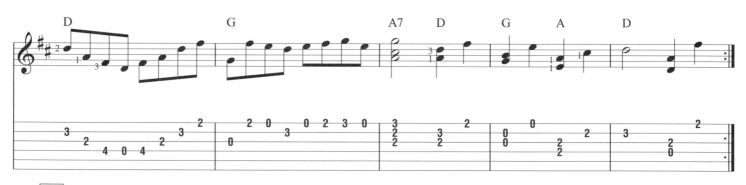

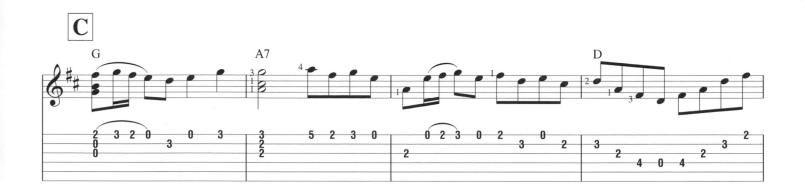

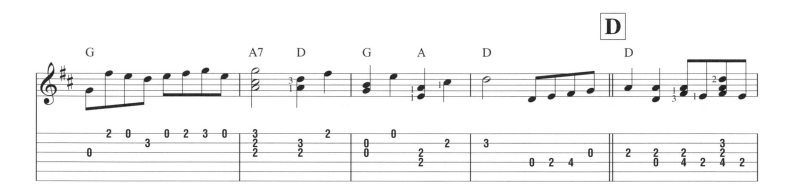

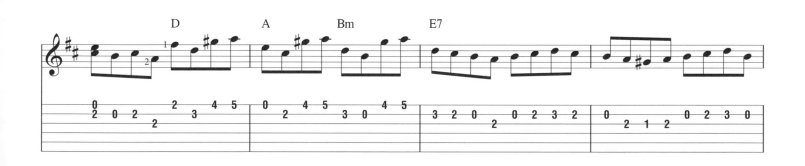

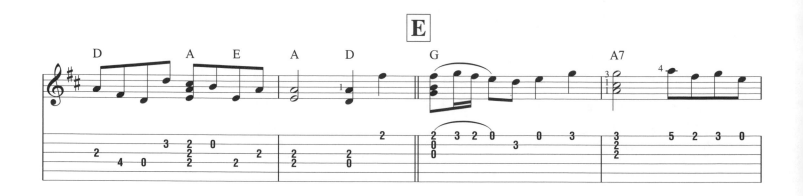

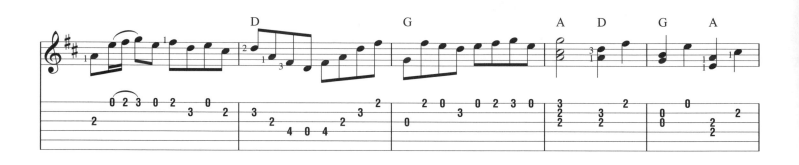

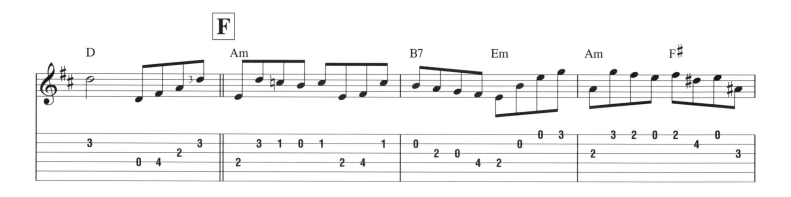

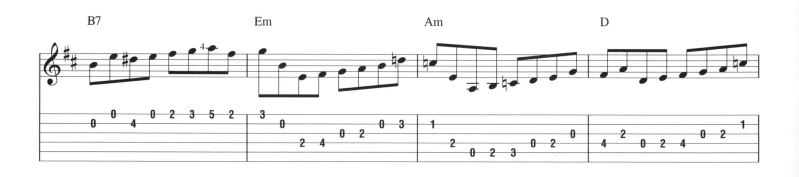

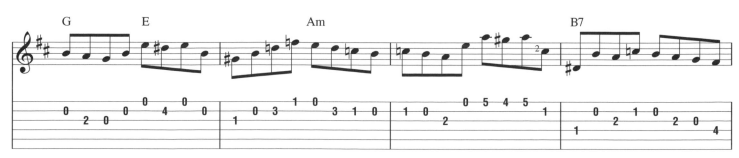

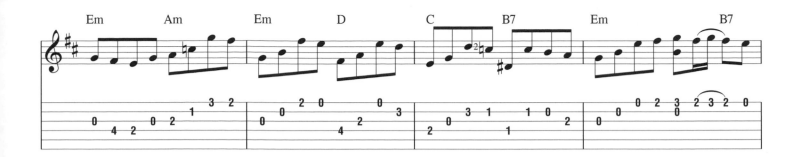

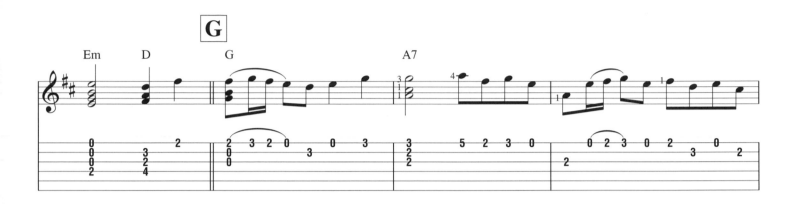

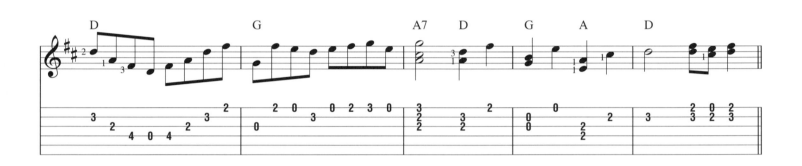

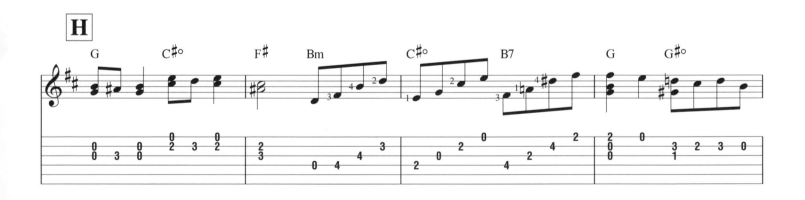

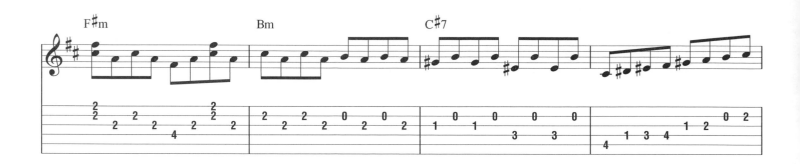

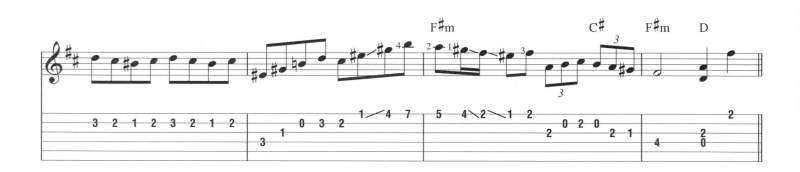

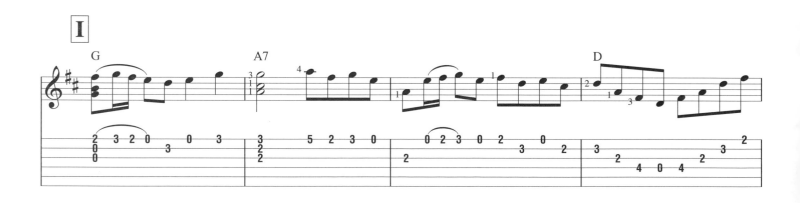

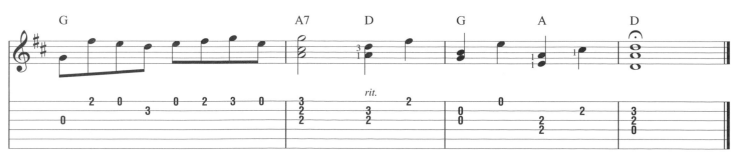

Prelude in C Major

from THE WELL-TEMPERED CLAVIER, BOOK 1

By Johann Sebastian Bach

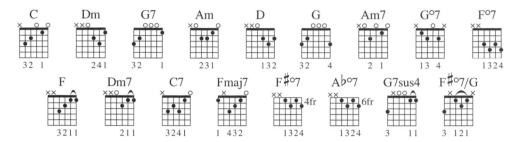

Strum Pattern: 2
Pick Pattern: 2

Moderately slow

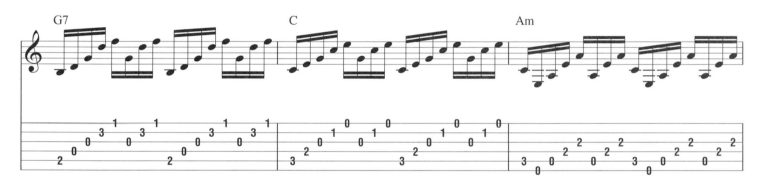

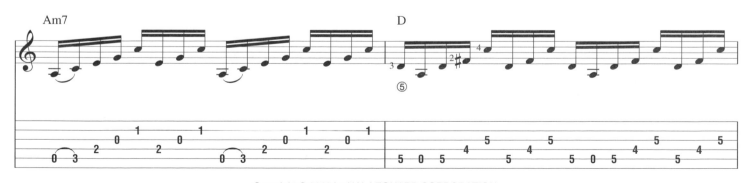

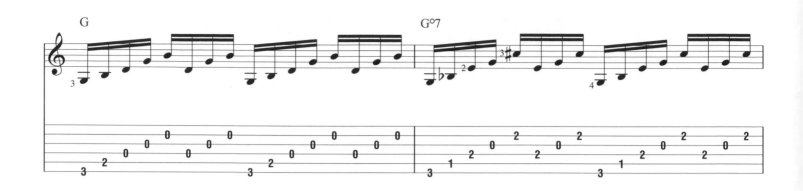

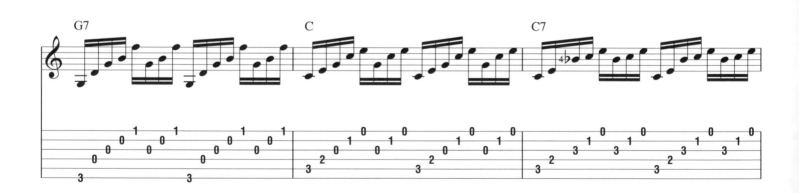

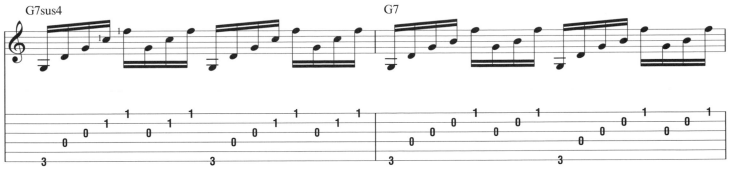

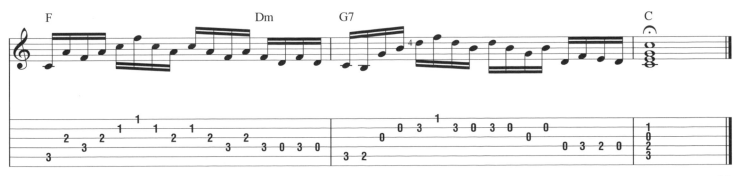

Jesu, Joy of Man's Desiring

By Johann Sebastian Bach

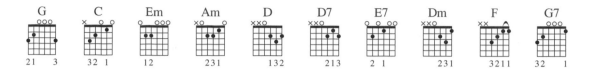

Strum Pattern: 8
Pick Pattern: 8

Intro
Moderately

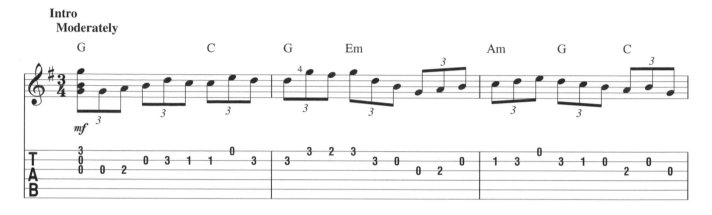

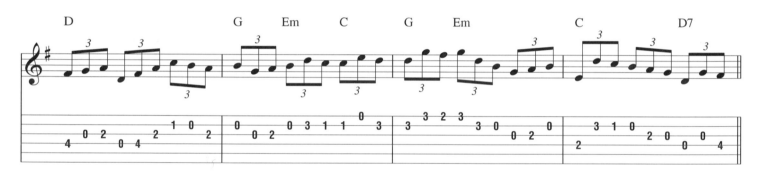

Verse

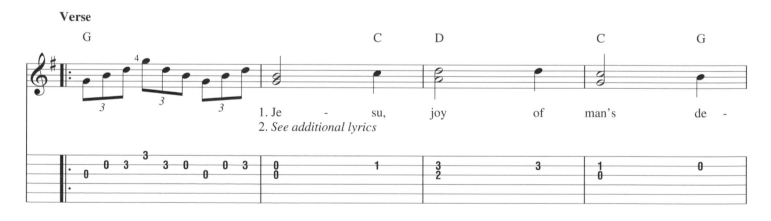

1. Je - su,   joy   of   man's   de -
2. *See additional lyrics*

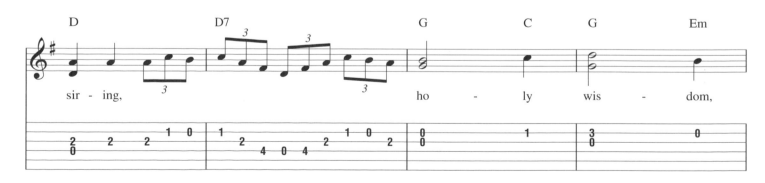

sir - ing,   ho - ly   wis - dom,

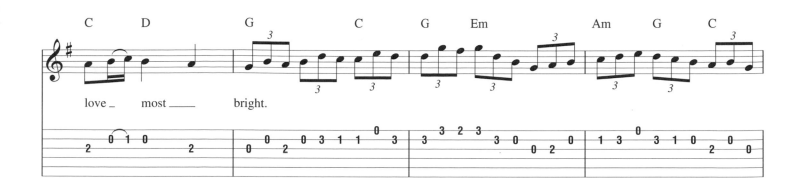

love _ most _____ bright.

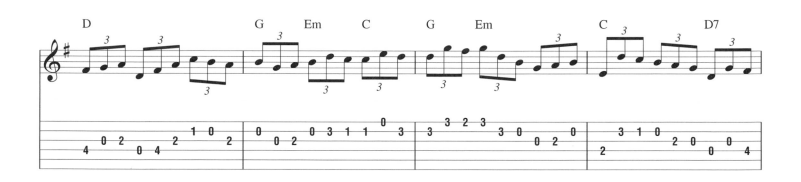

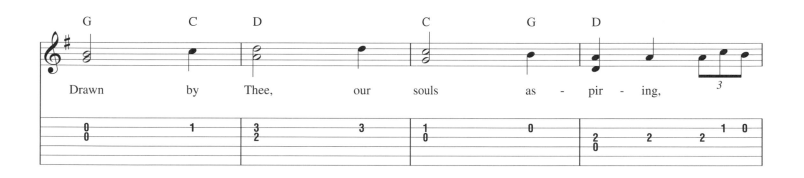

Drawn by Thee, our souls as - pir - ing,

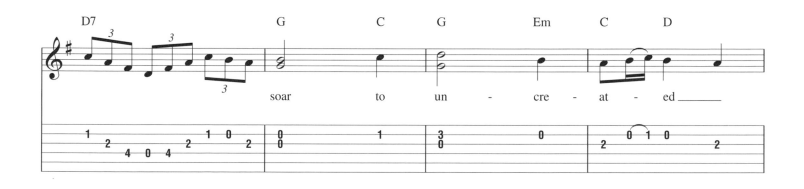

soar to un - cre - at - ed _____

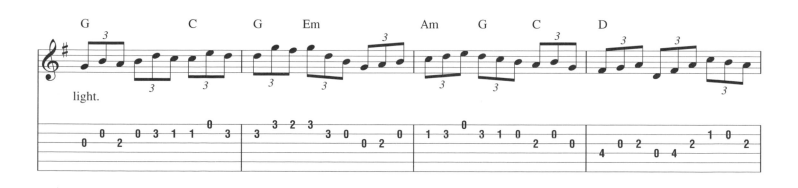

light.

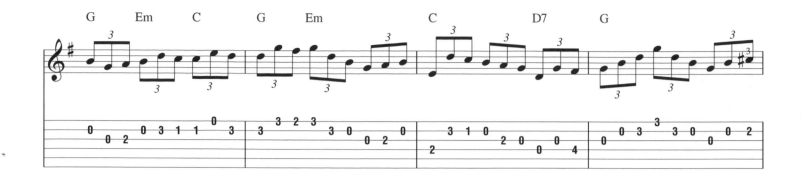

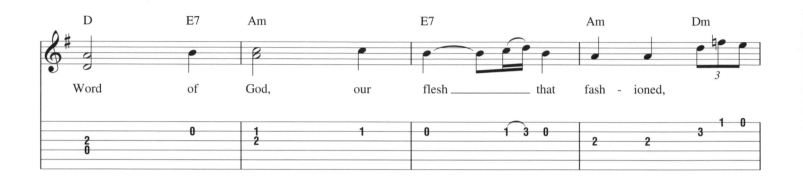

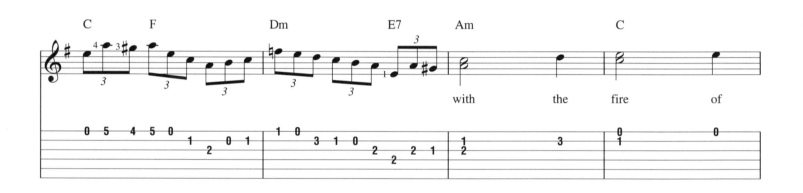

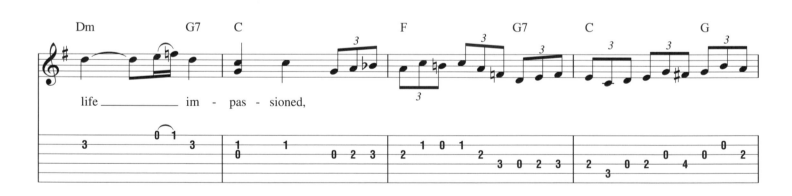

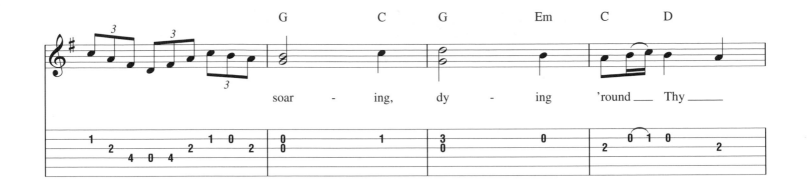

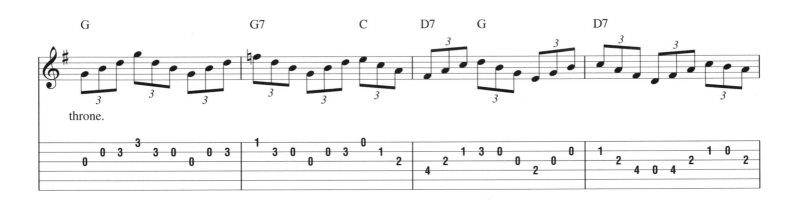

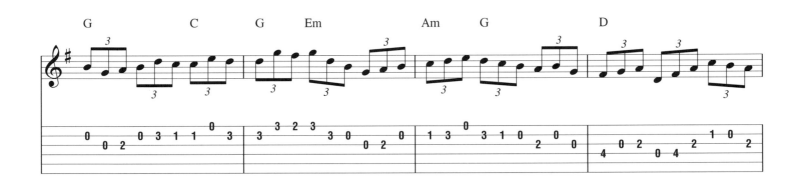

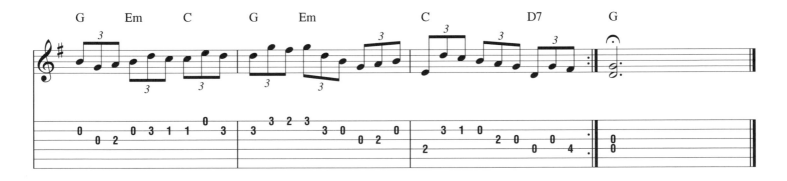

Additional Lyrics

2. Through the way where hope is guiding,
   Hark, what peaceful music rings!
   Where the flock in Thee confiding,
   Drink of joy from deathless springs.
   Their's is beauty's fairest pleasure,
   Their's is wisdom's holiest treasure.
   Thou dost ever lead Thine own,
   Is the love of joys unknown.

Little Prelude No. 2 in C Major

By Johann Sebastian Bach

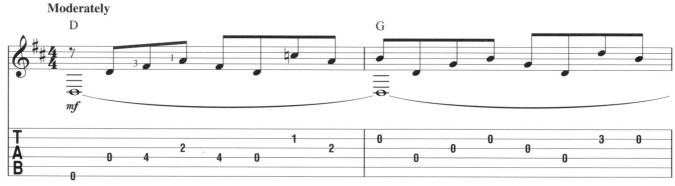

Drop D tuning, down 1 step:
(low to high) C-G-C-F-A-D

Strum Pattern: 4
Pick Pattern: 2

Moderately

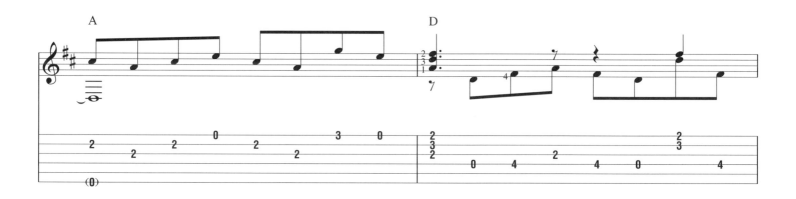

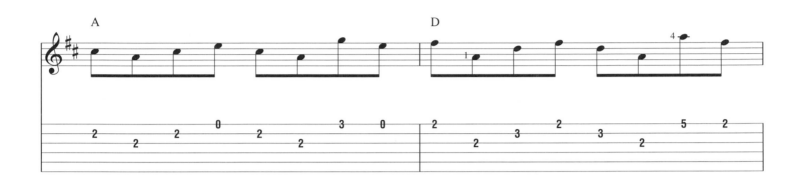

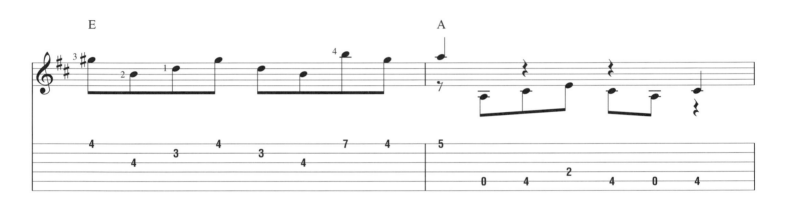

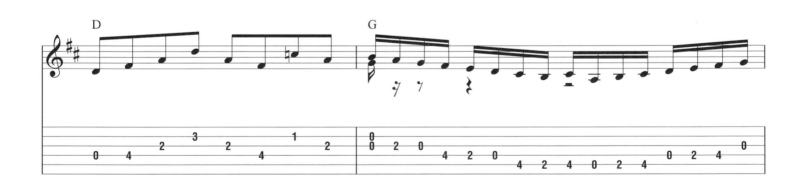

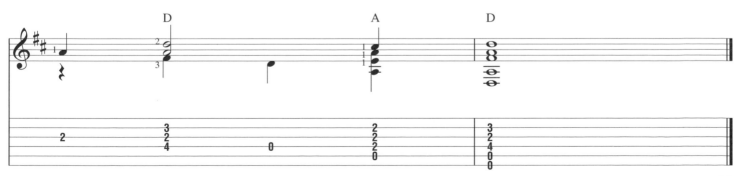

Minuet in G
(from the Anna Magdalena Notebook)

By Johann Sebastian Bach

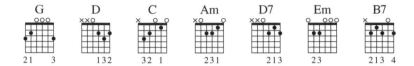

Strum Pattern: 8
Pick Pattern: 8

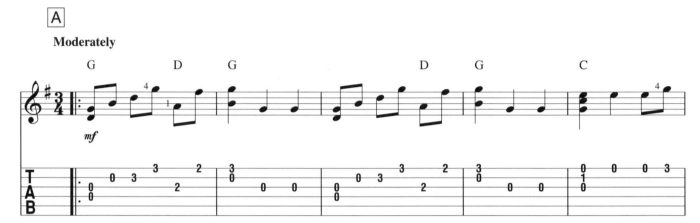

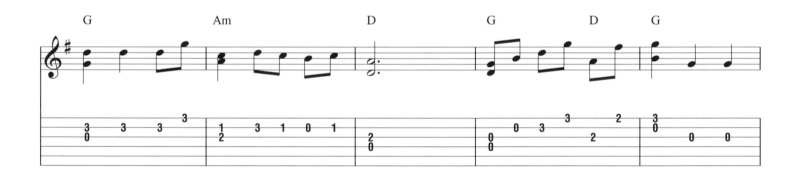

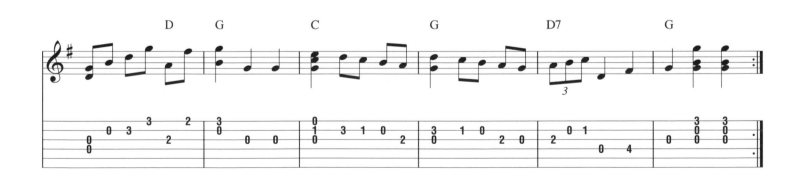

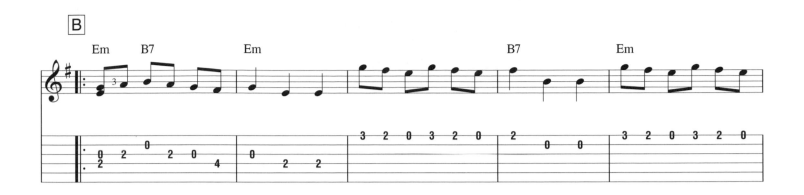

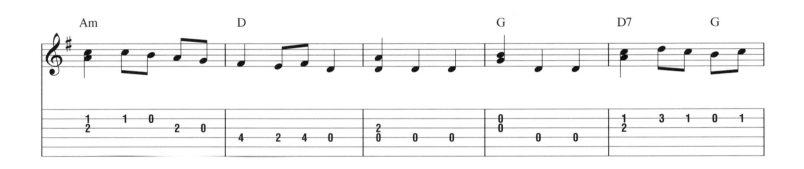

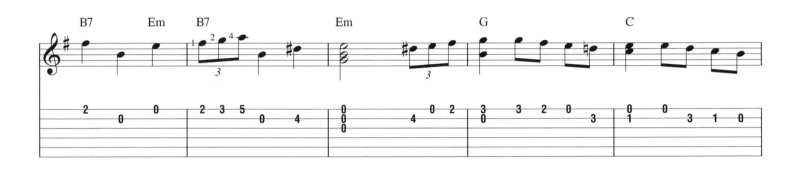

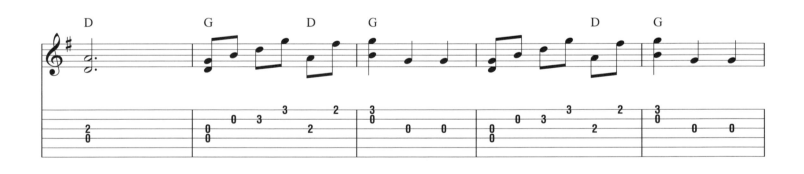

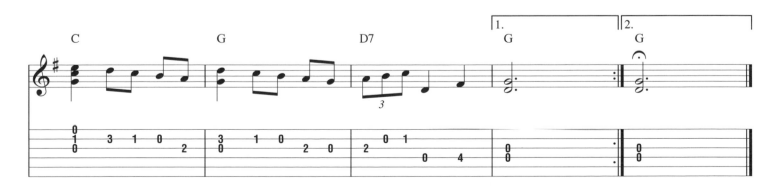

Prelude
(Cello Suite No. 1)
By Johann Sebastian Bach

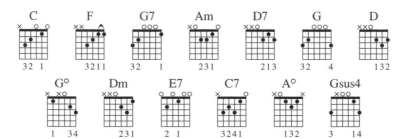

Strum Pattern: 3
Pick Pattern: 5

Moderately slow

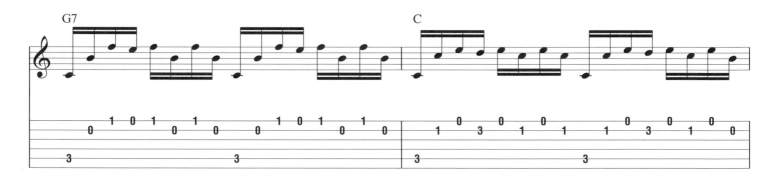

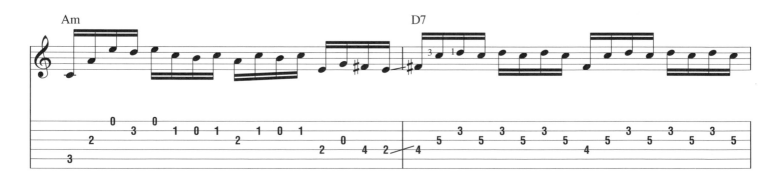

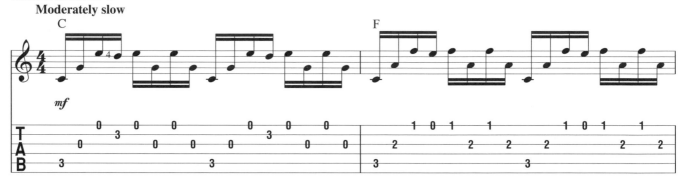

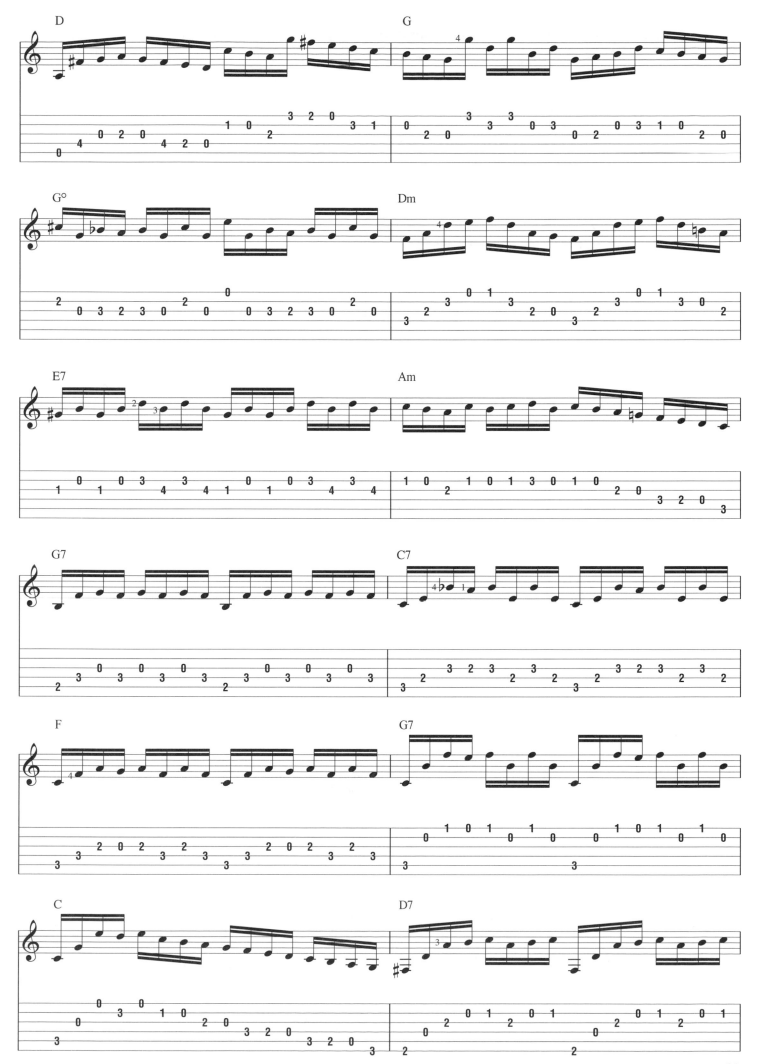

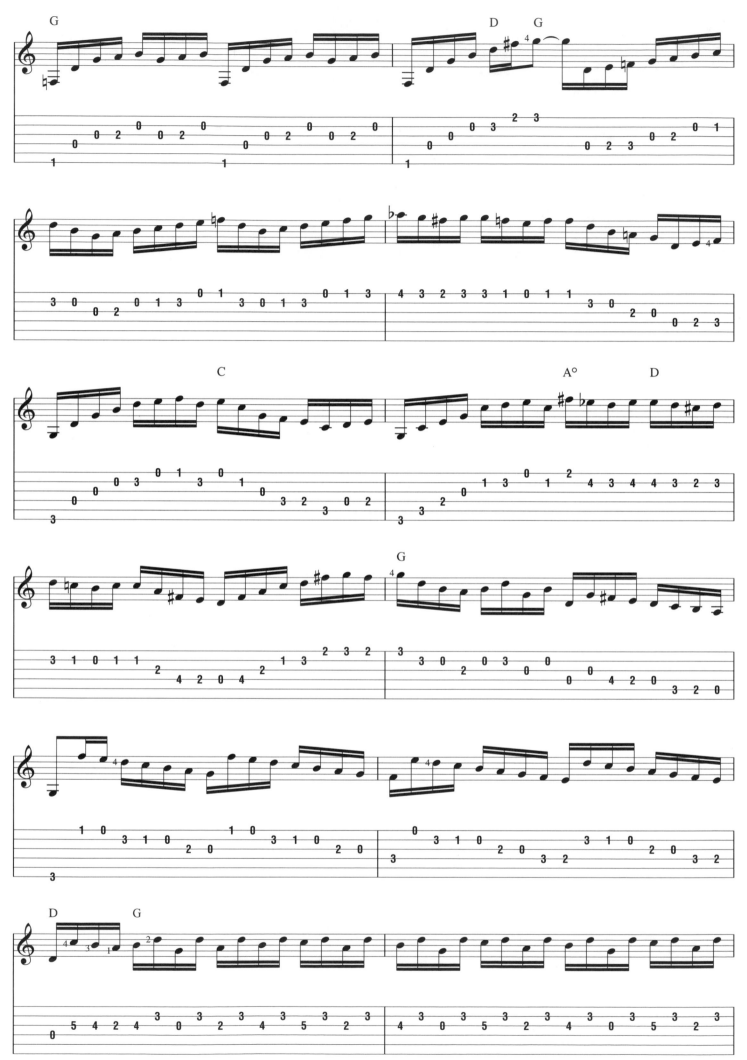

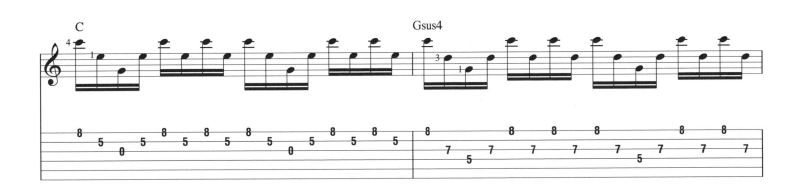

Sheep May Safely Graze

By Johann Sebastian Bach

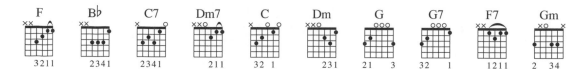

Strum Pattern: 3
Pick Pattern: 3

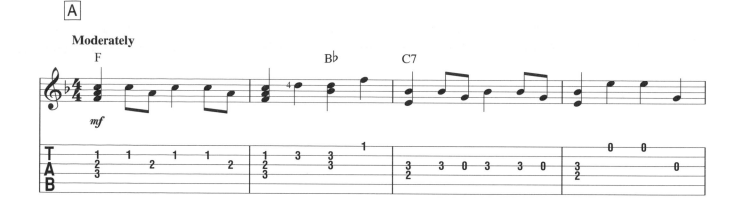

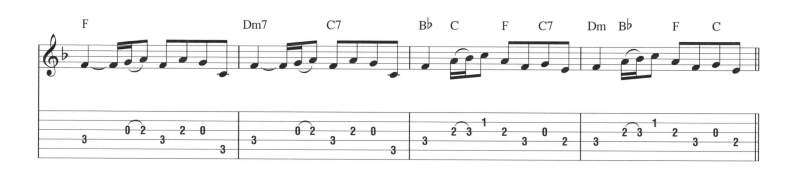

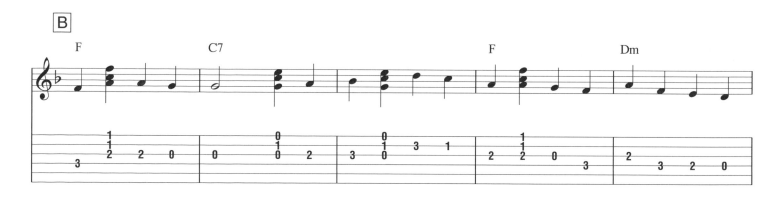

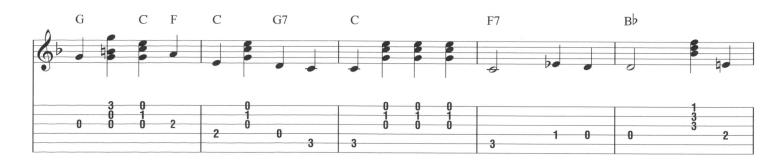

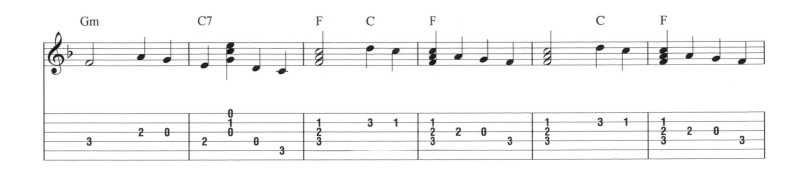

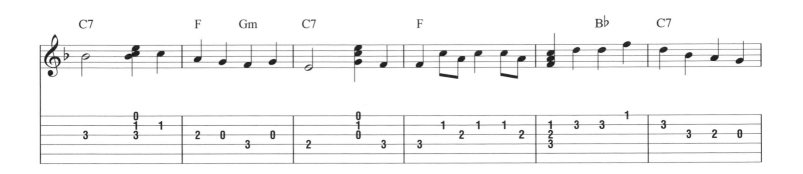

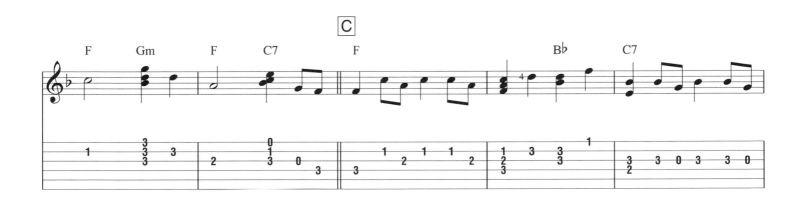

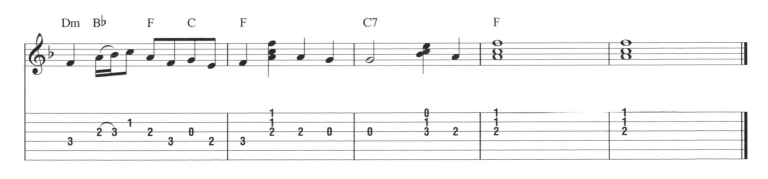

Siciliano

from SONATA NO. 2 FOR HARPSICHORD AND FLUTE

By Johann Sebastian Bach

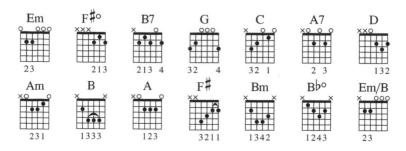

Strum Pattern: 9
Pick Pattern: 9

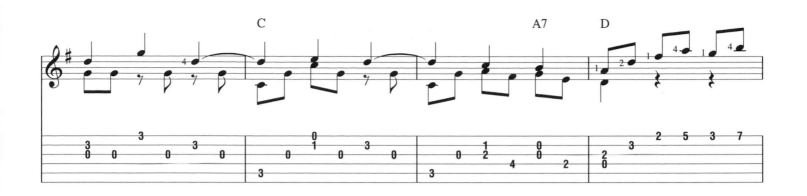

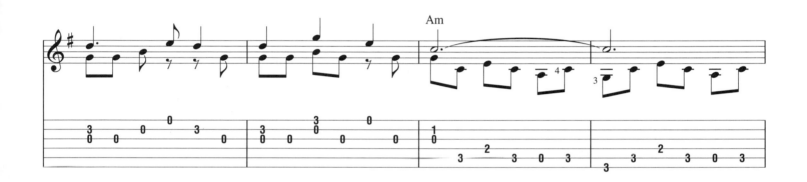

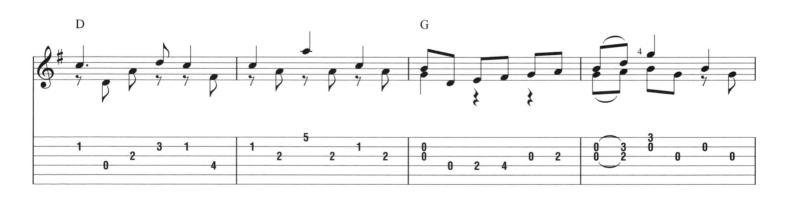

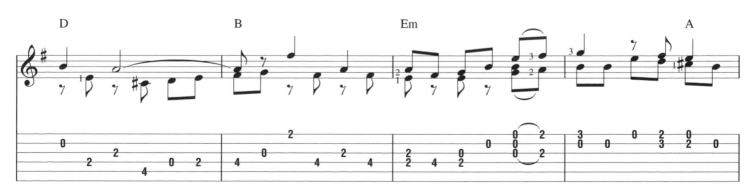

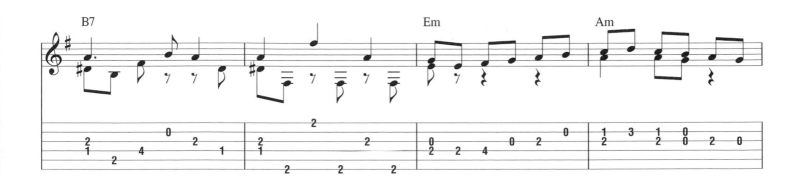

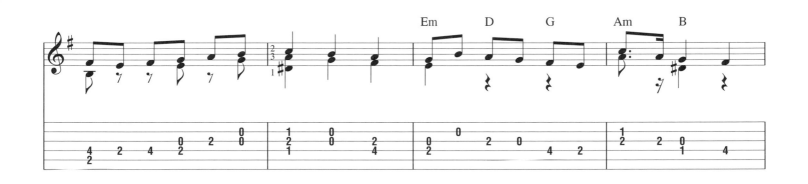

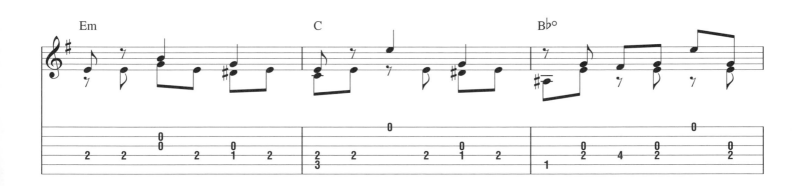

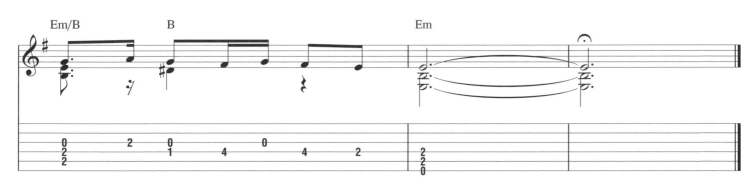

Sleepers, Awake

(Wachet Auf)

from CANTATA NO. 140

By Johann Sebastian Bach

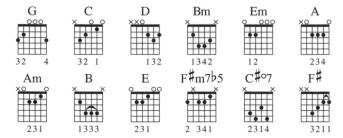

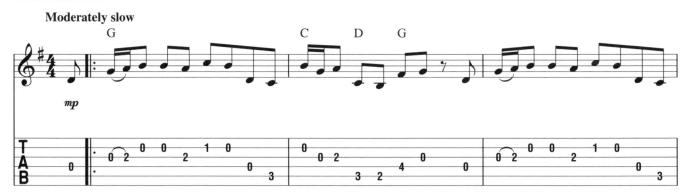

Strum Pattern: 4
Pick Pattern: 4

Moderately slow

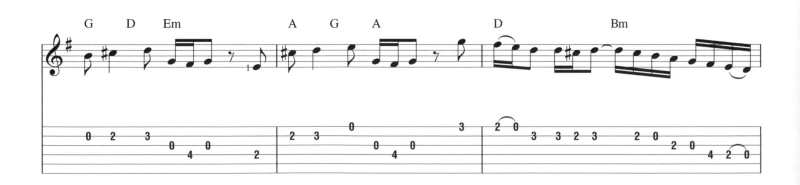

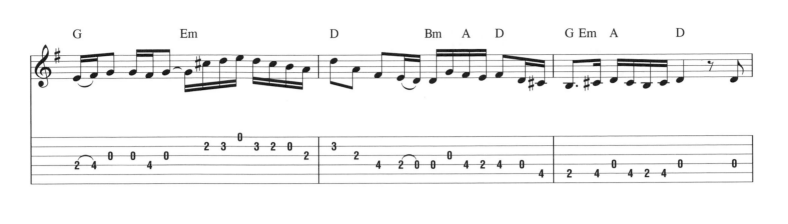

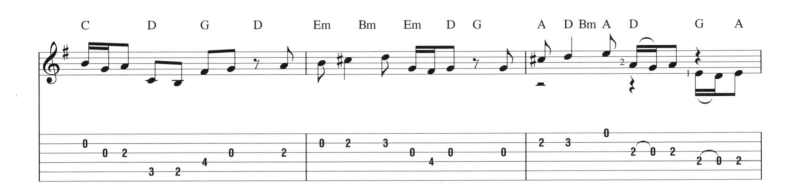

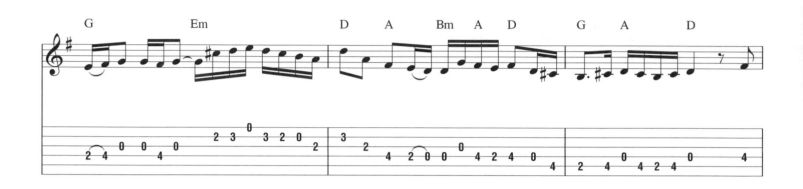

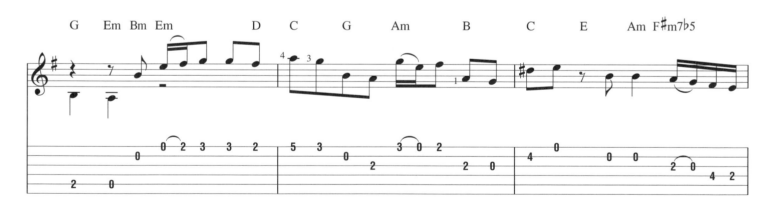

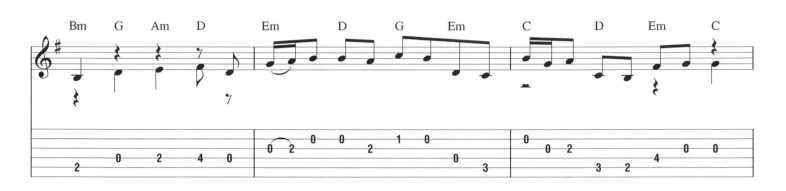

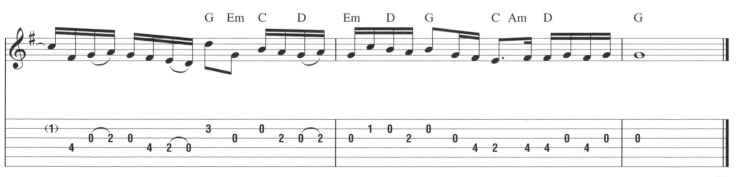

Quia Respexit

from MAGNIFICAT

By Johann Sebastian Bach

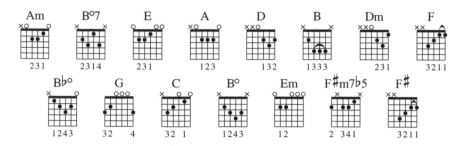

Strum Pattern: 3
Pick Pattern: 3

Moderately, in 2

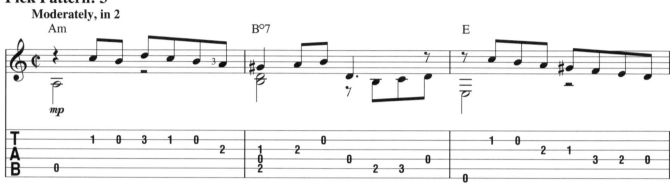

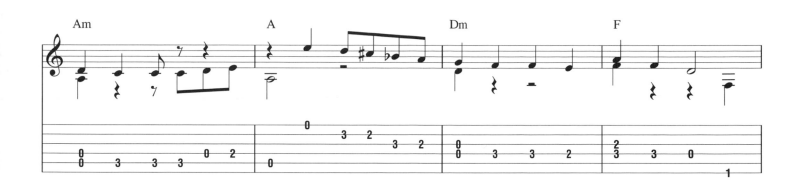

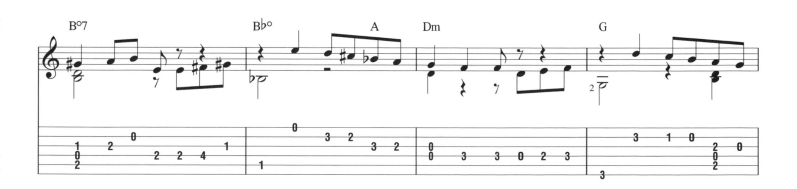

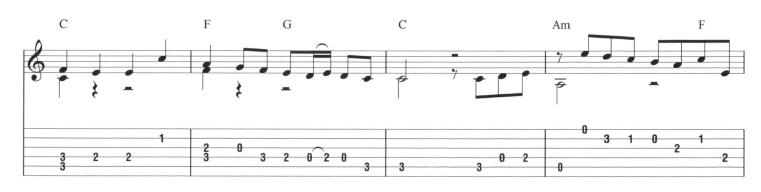

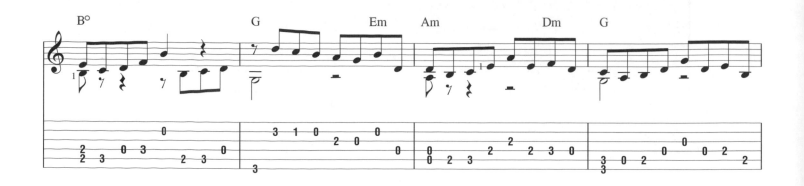

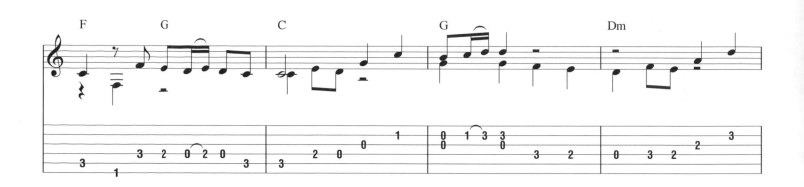

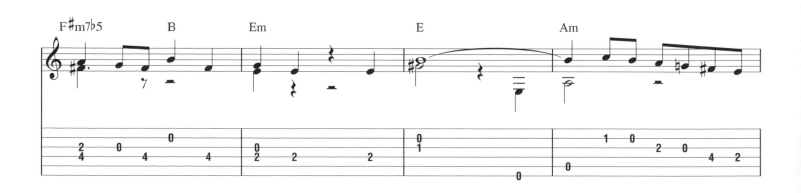